The Mercenary's Legacy: Tales of Honor, Duty and Sacrifice

Rolf Tucker

Table Of Contents

Chapter 1: Introduction to Mercenaries
and Private Military Contractors   3
    What are Mercenaries?   3
    History of Mercenaries   4
    Private Military Contractors (PMC)   6
    Current State of PMC Industry   7

Chapter 2: The Life of a Mercenary   9
    Recruitment and Training   9
    Deployment   11
    Combat and Survival   13

The Mercenary's Legacy: Tales of Honor, Duty and Sacrifice

Post-Deployment Life ... 15

Chapter 3: Tales of Honor ... 17
Acts of Valor ... 17

Going Above and Beyond ... 18

Selfless Sacrifices ... 20

Examples of Honor in the Field ... 21

Chapter 4: Duty Calls ... 23
Fulfilling the Mission ... 23

Loyalty to Country and Team ... 25

Ethical Dilemmas ... 26

    The Importance of Duty   28

Chapter 5: The Ultimate Sacrifice   **29**

    Fallen Mercenaries   30

    Memorializing the Fallen   31

    Impact on Families and Communities   33

    Legacy of Sacrifice   34

Chapter 6: The Future of the Mercenary Industry   **36**

    Changes in the Industry   36

    Regulation and Oversight   38

    Advancements in Technology   40

    Opportunities and Challenges   42

The Mercenary's Legacy: Tales of Honor, Duty and Sacrifice

Chapter 7: Conclusion: Reflections on the Legacy of Mercenaries — 43

- The Role of Mercenaries in History — 43
- Lessons Learned from Mercenaries — 45
- The Future of Mercenaries — 47
- The Legacy of Mercenaries in Society. — 49

Chapter 1: Introduction to Mercenaries and Private Military Contractors

What are Mercenaries?

What are Mercenaries?

Mercenaries are soldiers who are hired by a country or organization to fight in a conflict in exchange for monetary or other rewards. These fighters are not part of the regular military and do not fight for a specific country or cause. Instead, they are independent contractors who offer their services to the highest bidder.

The use of mercenaries dates back to ancient times, where they were often utilized by rulers as a way to supplement their armies in times of war. In the modern era, mercenaries have become increasingly prevalent, particularly in conflicts where the regular military is unable or unwilling to intervene.

Private military contractors (PMC) are a type of mercenary that has gained significant attention in recent years. These companies offer a wide range of services, including security, logistics, and intelligence gathering.

While mercenaries can be highly effective fighters, they also come with a number of risks and challenges. One of the main concerns is that they may lack the loyalty and discipline of regular soldiers, as they are motivated primarily by money rather than a sense of duty or allegiance.

Additionally, mercenaries may not be subject to the same rules of engagement and standards of behavior as regular soldiers. This can lead to ethical and legal concerns, particularly when it comes to issues such as the treatment of prisoners and civilians.

Despite these challenges, the use of mercenaries is likely to remain a prevalent feature of modern warfare. As conflicts become increasingly complex and the lines between state and non-state actors become blurred, the need for agile and flexible military forces is likely to grow.

Overall, while the use of mercenaries may be controversial, it is clear that they play an important role in modern warfare. Whether they are viewed as heroes or villains, mercenaries continue to shape the course of history through their actions on the battlefield.

History of Mercenaries

The history of mercenaries can be traced back to ancient times when mercenaries were hired to fight in wars that were not their own. Mercenaries were often used when a nation's army was too small or when a ruler did not want to risk the lives of their own soldiers. These mercenaries were often free men who were willing to fight for pay and loot.

During the Middle Ages, mercenaries played a significant role in the wars between European nations. Mercenaries were often hired by the highest bidder, and they would fight for the side that paid them the most. Mercenaries were also used by rulers as personal guards and for other duties.

The use of mercenaries declined during the Renaissance, but they resurfaced during the 17th and 18th centuries. Mercenaries were used by European nations to fight in their colonies in Africa, the Americas, and Asia. These mercenaries were often recruited from other countries and were known for their brutality and lack of loyalty.

The 19th and 20th centuries saw the rise of the modern mercenary. Mercenaries were hired by private companies and individuals to provide security and protection. They were used in conflicts around the world, including in Africa, the Middle East, and Latin America. Private military contractors (PMC) also emerged during this time, providing military services to governments and private companies.

The use of mercenaries and PMCs has been controversial, with many critics arguing that they undermine the authority of governments and contribute to instability in conflict zones. However, proponents of the use of mercenaries argue that they provide a necessary service and that they are often more effective than traditional military forces.

Despite the controversy surrounding mercenaries and PMCs, they continue to play a significant role in modern warfare. The legacy of the mercenary is one of honor, duty, and sacrifice, with many mercenaries risking their lives for the sake of others. The stories of these brave men and women serve as a reminder of the sacrifices made by those who have served as mercenaries throughout history.

Private Military Contractors (PMC)

The Mercenary's Legacy: Tales of Honor, Duty and Sacrifice

The use of Private Military Contractors (PMC) has become increasingly popular in modern conflicts. These contractors are individuals or groups hired by governments, corporations, or other organizations to provide military services. PMC's are also known as mercenaries, and they are seen as a cost-effective and efficient alternative to traditional military forces.

PMC's have been used in many conflicts around the world, including Iraq, Afghanistan, and Syria. They provide a range of services, including security, logistics, training, and intelligence gathering. PMC's also operate in high-risk environments, such as war zones, where traditional military forces may not be able to operate effectively.

The Mercenary's Legacy: Tales of Honor, Duty and Sacrifice

One of the advantages of using PMC's is their flexibility. They can be hired for short-term or long-term contracts, and they can be deployed quickly to areas where they are needed. PMC's are also able to adapt to changing situations and can provide specialized services that traditional military forces may not have the capacity to provide.

However, the use of PMC's is not without controversy. Critics argue that they are not accountable to the same level as traditional military forces. PMC's are not subject to the same legal frameworks as regular soldiers, and there have been cases of human rights abuses and other illegal activities.

Despite these concerns, the use of PMC's is likely to continue. As governments and corporations seek to reduce costs and increase efficiency, PMC's will remain an attractive option. However, it is important that the use of PMC's is regulated and that they are held accountable for their actions.

The Mercenary's Legacy: Tales of Honor, Duty and Sacrifice

In conclusion, the use of Private Military Contractors (PMC) is a complex and controversial issue. While they provide many benefits, such as flexibility and cost-effectiveness, there are also concerns about their accountability and legality. It is important that the use of PMC's is regulated and that they are held to the same standards as traditional military forces. As the world becomes increasingly complex and dangerous, PMC's will continue to be an important part of the military landscape, but their use must be carefully managed and monitored.

Current State of PMC Industry

The private military contractor (PMC) industry has been in existence for several decades, but it has only gained significant attention in recent years. This industry is made up of private companies that offer military services to governments, corporations, and individuals for a fee. The industry has grown exponentially in the past decade, with an estimated worth of $200 billion in 2021.

The current state of the PMC industry is one of growth and change. The industry has faced increasing scrutiny for its operations in conflict zones, particularly in the Middle East. The use of contractors in Iraq and Afghanistan led to controversy over the lack of accountability for their actions, particularly in instances of civilian casualties.

In response, many governments have increased regulations on the use of contractors, particularly in combat roles. The United States, for example, has implemented strict rules on the use of contractors in combat zones. This has led to a shift in the industry, with many companies focusing on providing logistics and support services to military operations rather than direct combat roles.

The industry has also seen a shift towards greater specialization. Many companies now focus on specific areas of military expertise, such as cybersecurity or intelligence gathering. This has led to a more competitive industry, with companies vying for contracts based on their specialized skills.

Despite the controversies surrounding the industry, the demand for PMC services continues to grow. Many governments lack the resources to provide their own military services, particularly in areas of conflict. Private companies can fill this gap, providing essential services to support military operations.

Overall, the current state of the PMC industry is one of growth and change. The industry has faced controversies and regulations, but it continues to provide essential services to governments and corporations around the world. As the industry evolves, it will be essential to maintain accountability and transparency to ensure that contractors operate within the bounds of international law and human rights standards.

Chapter 2: The Life of a Mercenary

Recruitment and Training

Recruitment and Training

One of the most critical aspects of any successful mercenary or private military contractor (PMC) operation is the recruitment and training of personnel. Unlike traditional military forces, mercenaries and PMCs are made up of individuals from a wide range of backgrounds, including former military personnel, law enforcement officers, and civilians with specialized skills.

Recruitment

The first step in building a successful mercenary or PMC team is finding the right people for the job. This requires a thorough understanding of the specific skills and experience needed for the mission at hand, as well as the ability to identify individuals who are reliable, trustworthy, and capable of working well in a high-pressure, high-stakes environment.

One of the most effective ways to recruit personnel for a mercenary or PMC operation is through personal networks. Many experienced mercenaries and PMCs have extensive networks of contacts in the military, law enforcement, and other areas of expertise, which can be leveraged to find the right people for the job.

In addition to personal networks, many mercenary and PMC companies also rely on recruitment agencies and online job boards to find qualified candidates. These resources can be particularly useful for identifying individuals with specialized skills or experience in areas such as intelligence gathering, logistics, and medical support.

Training

Once the right personnel have been recruited, the next step is to provide them with the training they need to succeed in the mission at hand. This may involve a combination of classroom instruction, hands-on training exercises, and simulations designed to replicate real-world scenarios.

Training for mercenary and PMC personnel typically covers a wide range of topics, including weapons handling, tactical operations, first aid, language and cultural awareness, and communication and teamwork skills. In addition, personnel may receive specialized training in areas such as close protection, surveillance, or cyber security, depending on the specific needs of the mission.

One of the key advantages of mercenary and PMC companies is their ability to provide highly specialized training tailored to the unique needs of each client. This can include training on specific weapons systems, tactics, and procedures, as well as cultural and language training to help personnel operate effectively in different parts of the world.

Conclusion

Recruitment and training are critical components of any successful mercenary or PMC operation. By identifying and recruiting the right personnel, and providing them with the training they need to succeed in their mission, mercenary and PMC companies can ensure that they are able to deliver the highest level of performance and security to their clients.

Deployment

Deployment is the most critical stage in the life of a mercenary. It is the moment when he or she transitions from civilian life to the battlefield, putting their lives on the line in service to their country or for a private client. The deployment phase is a complex process that requires careful planning, preparation, and execution. In this subchapter, we will explore the deployment phase of a mercenary's mission, its challenges, and how to overcome them.

The deployment phase begins with the selection of the right team for the mission. A mercenary's team comprises of individuals with different skills, and their selection depends on the nature of the mission. The team must be trained to operate in hostile environments, have excellent communication skills, and be physically fit. Their equipment must also be in good condition to ensure they can complete their mission successfully.

The next step is the pre-deployment phase. This phase involves getting all the necessary paperwork and approvals from the client or the contracting agency. The team must also undergo medical checkups and receive vaccinations to prevent diseases that are prevalent in the deployment area. During this phase, the team also receives briefings on the mission objective, the terrain, and the potential threats they might face.

The deployment phase itself is the most challenging and dangerous phase of the mission. The team must always be alert and ready to respond to any threats. The team leader must ensure that all members understand their roles and responsibilities and work together as a cohesive unit. The team must also maintain good communication with the client or the contracting agency to keep them informed of their progress.

After the mission is complete, the team must undergo the post-deployment phase. This phase involves debriefing, medical checkups, and decompression to help the team recover from the stress and trauma of the mission. The team leader must also ensure that all the equipment is returned in good condition, and the paperwork is completed.

In conclusion, the deployment phase is the most critical stage in the life of a mercenary. It is a complex process that requires careful planning, preparation, and execution. The team must be well-trained, physically fit, and have excellent communication skills. The deployment phase is also the most dangerous and challenging phase of the mission, and the team must always be alert and ready to respond to any threats. The post-deployment phase is also essential to help the team recover from the stress of the mission. In all, the deployment phase is not for the faint-hearted, and only the best-prepared teams can survive and complete their mission successfully.

Combat and Survival

Combat and Survival

Combat and survival are two sides of the same coin for mercenaries and private military contractors (PMC). The ability to fight and win battles, and to survive in hostile environments, are essential skills for anyone who works in this line of work. In this chapter, we will explore some of the key techniques, strategies, and tools that are used by mercenaries and PMC contractors to survive and succeed in combat.

One of the most important skills for any combatant is marksmanship. The ability to shoot accurately and effectively is critical in any battle. Mercenaries and PMC contractors are often trained to use a variety of weapons, including rifles, pistols, and machine guns. They learn how to aim, shoot, and reload quickly and accurately, even under extreme stress.

Another key skill for survival in combat is physical fitness. Mercenaries and PMC contractors must be in top physical condition in order to endure the rigors of battle. This includes strength training, endurance exercises, and mental conditioning. A strong mind and body are essential for surviving in the field.

In addition to physical fitness, mercenaries and PMC contractors must also be mentally tough. They must be able to withstand the stress and pressure of combat, and to remain focused and alert at all times. They must also be able to adapt quickly to changing situations and make split-second decisions that could mean the difference between life and death.

One of the most important tools for survival in combat is communication. Mercenaries and PMC contractors must be able to communicate effectively with each other, even in the midst of battle. They use radios, hand signals, and other forms of communication to coordinate their movements and tactics.

Finally, survival in combat often depends on the ability to blend in with the local environment. Mercenaries and PMC contractors must be able to move stealthily, avoid detection, and blend in with the local population. They may wear local clothing, speak the local language, and use other techniques to stay hidden and avoid detection.

In conclusion, combat and survival are essential skills for anyone who works as a mercenary or PMC contractor. By mastering marksmanship, physical fitness, mental toughness, communication, and stealth, these professionals are able to survive and succeed in even the most hostile environments.

Post-Deployment Life

Post-Deployment Life

The life of a mercenary or private military contractor (PMC) is one that is filled with adventure and excitement, but it is also one that is fraught with danger and uncertainty. After a deployment, the transition back to civilian life can be a difficult one. Many mercenaries struggle with the aftermath of war, including PTSD, physical injuries, and emotional trauma.

One of the biggest challenges that mercenaries face when they return home is finding a sense of purpose and meaning in their lives. For many, the adrenaline rush of combat is hard to replace, and they may find themselves feeling bored or unfulfilled in their civilian lives. It is important for these individuals to find new challenges and pursuits that give them a sense of purpose and fulfillment.

Another challenge that many mercenaries face is rejoining society after spending months or even years in a combat zone. They may find it difficult to relate to others who have not experienced the same things they have, and they may struggle to readjust to the pace of civilian life. It is important for these individuals to seek out support from other veterans and to find ways to connect with their communities.

One of the most significant challenges that mercenaries face after a deployment is dealing with the physical and emotional toll that combat takes on their bodies and minds. Many veterans struggle with PTSD, depression, and other mental health issues. It is important for these individuals to seek out professional help and to find ways to manage their symptoms.

Despite the challenges that come with post-deployment life, many mercenaries find that their experiences have given them a unique perspective on the world. They may find that their skills and experiences are highly valued in the private sector, and they may be able to find fulfilling careers in fields such as security, law enforcement, or disaster response.

In the end, the key to a successful post-deployment life for a mercenary or PMC is to find a sense of purpose and fulfillment, to seek out support from others who have shared their experiences, and to take care of their physical and emotional health. With the right mindset and support, these individuals can go on to lead rich and fulfilling lives long after their deployments have ended.

Chapter 3: Tales of Honor

Acts of Valor

Acts of Valor

In the world of mercenaries and private military contractors (PMC), acts of valor are common occurrences. These brave men and women put their lives on the line every day in the pursuit of honor, duty, and sacrifice. They are often called upon to undertake dangerous missions in some of the most inhospitable places on earth.

Acts of valor are defined as actions in which a person exhibits exceptional courage, bravery, or selflessness in the face of extreme danger. These actions can take many forms, from saving the lives of fellow soldiers to completing a mission that seemed impossible.

One example of an act of valor occurred in the deserts of Iraq. A group of private military contractors was tasked with protecting a convoy of trucks carrying vital supplies to a remote military base. As they drove through the desert, they were ambushed by a group of heavily armed insurgents.

Despite being outnumbered and outgunned, the contractors fought back with everything they had. They used their training and expertise to hold off the attackers long enough for the convoy to escape. Several of them were wounded in the fight, but they refused to give up, continuing to fight until the last of the insurgents had been eliminated.

Another example of an act of valor occurred in the mountains of Afghanistan. A group of mercenaries was tasked with rescuing a group of hostages who had been taken by a local warlord. The hostages were being held in a remote mountain fortress, surrounded by heavily armed guards.

The mercenaries knew that the mission was almost certainly a suicide mission, but they refused to back down. They launched a daring assault on the fortress, using their skills and training to overcome the guards and free the hostages. Several of the mercenaries were killed in the fierce fighting, but they had accomplished their mission and saved the lives of innocent civilians.

Acts of valor are not just limited to combat situations. They can also occur in everyday life, as people put themselves at risk to help others. For example, a private military contractor might risk their own safety to rescue a local civilian from a burning building, or to provide medical aid to someone in need.

In the world of mercenaries and private military contractors, acts of valor are an everyday occurrence. These brave men and women are willing to put themselves in harm's way to protect others and to uphold the values of honor, duty, and sacrifice. Their stories are a testament to the courage and dedication of those who serve in this unique and challenging profession.

Going Above and Beyond

Going Above and Beyond

As a mercenary or private military contractor (PMC), you are often called upon to perform tasks that go beyond the ordinary. You are expected to be able to handle any situation that arises, no matter how difficult or dangerous it may be. This is why going above and beyond is such an important part of your job.

Going above and beyond means doing more than what is expected of you. It means putting in extra effort to ensure that a mission is successful, even if it means taking on additional risks. This is not something that everyone is capable of, but it is something that mercenaries and PMCs excel at.

One of the key ways that you can go above and beyond is by being proactive. Instead of waiting for orders, take the initiative to identify potential threats and come up with solutions to address them. This may involve scouting out an area before a mission, or taking steps to secure a perimeter to prevent enemy infiltration.

Another way to go above and beyond is by being adaptable. Things don't always go according to plan, and when they don't, you need to be able to adjust quickly. This may mean changing tactics mid-mission, or coming up with a new plan on the fly.

Of course, going above and beyond also means being willing to take on extra risks. This may involve volunteering for a dangerous mission, or putting yourself in harm's way to protect others. While this can be challenging, it is also what sets mercenaries and PMCs apart from other military personnel.

Ultimately, going above and beyond is about demonstrating a commitment to your mission and your colleagues. It requires a willingness to put yourself on the line for the greater good, and to do whatever it takes to ensure that your team is successful. This is what makes mercenaries and PMCs such valuable assets, and why they are trusted to take on some of the most challenging missions in the world.

Selfless Sacrifices

Selfless Sacrifices

In the world of mercenaries and private military contractors (PMC), sacrifices are a common occurrence. These men and women often put their lives on the line to protect their clients, fulfill their duties, and uphold their honor. Selfless sacrifices are a hallmark of their profession, and they go above and beyond the call of duty to ensure the success of their missions.

One such story of selfless sacrifice is that of a PMC team that was tasked with protecting a high-ranking government official on a diplomatic mission to a war-torn country. The team consisted of seasoned veterans who had seen it all, but the mission would test their skills and bravery to the limit.

During the mission, the team encountered heavy resistance from insurgents who were determined to disrupt the peace talks. Despite the danger, the team pressed on, using their training and experience to overcome the enemy's tactics. However, during a particularly intense firefight, one of the team members was critically injured.

The injured team member was unable to move, and the team was faced with a difficult decision. They could leave him behind and continue the mission, or they could stay behind and risk their own lives to save him. Without hesitation, the team decided to stay behind and do everything in their power to save their comrade.

For several hours, the team fought off the enemy while also providing medical aid to their injured teammate. They worked together, using their skills and resources to keep him alive until a rescue team arrived. The team's selfless sacrifice saved their comrade's life and proved that they were not just hired guns, but also honorable and compassionate individuals.

This story is just one example of the many selfless sacrifices made by mercenaries and PMC contractors. These brave men and women put their lives on the line every day to protect their clients, fulfill their duties, and uphold their honor. Their sacrifices are a testament to their dedication, bravery, and unwavering commitment to their profession.

In conclusion, selfless sacrifices are an essential part of the mercenary and PMC profession. They are a testament to the courage and honor of these individuals, who put their lives on the line to protect others. Their stories serve as an inspiration to us all, reminding us that even in the darkest of times, there are still individuals willing to make selfless sacrifices for the greater good.

Examples of Honor in the Field

Examples of Honor in the Field

As mercenaries and private military contractors (PMC), the men and women who serve in these roles often operate in environments that are far from the comforts of home. They may find themselves in conflict zones, providing security for important personnel, or guarding critical infrastructure. Despite the challenges they face, many of these individuals are driven by a strong sense of honor, duty, and sacrifice. Here are just a few examples of honor in action in the field.

One of the most famous examples of mercenary honor is that of Bob Denard. Denard was a French mercenary who fought in several African conflicts, including the Congo Crisis, the Angolan Civil War, and the Comoros Crisis. Despite his controversial actions, Denard was regarded by many of his fellow mercenaries as a man of honor. He was known for his loyalty to his comrades and his willingness to risk his own life to protect them.

The Mercenary's Legacy: Tales of Honor, Duty and Sacrifice

Another example of honor in the field is that of private military contractor Tim Spicer. Spicer is a former British Army officer who founded the PMC Aegis Defense Services. In 2004, Spicer and his team were responsible for providing security for the Iraqi Oil Ministry during the height of the insurgency. Despite facing constant danger, Spicer refused to abandon his post, even when ordered to do so by his superiors. His actions helped prevent a major oil crisis in Iraq and earned him the respect of his colleagues.

Finally, there is the story of the Blackwater contractors who were killed and mutilated in Fallujah, Iraq, in 2004. Despite the horrific nature of the attack, the surviving contractors refused to abandon their fallen comrades. They risked their own lives to retrieve the bodies of their fallen brothers, demonstrating the kind of honor and loyalty that is all too rare in today's world.

These are just a few examples of the kind of honor that can be found in the field of mercenaries and private military contractors. Despite the negative stereotypes that often surround these professions, many men and women who serve in these roles are driven by a strong sense of duty, sacrifice, and honor. Their actions serve as a powerful reminder of the importance of these values, not just in the field of conflict, but in all areas of life.

Chapter 4: Duty Calls

Fulfilling the Mission

Fulfilling the Mission

For mercenaries and private military contractors (PMC), fulfilling the mission is not just a job—it's a way of life. These individuals are often called upon to perform some of the most difficult and dangerous tasks in the world, and they do so with honor, duty, and sacrifice. But what does it mean to fulfill the mission, and how can you ensure that you are doing so to the best of your ability?

At its core, fulfilling the mission means completing the task at hand, no matter how difficult or dangerous it may be. For mercenaries and PMC contractors, this can mean everything from providing security for high-profile individuals to engaging in combat operations in hostile environments. But beyond simply completing the task, fulfilling the mission also means doing so with honor and integrity.

This means adhering to a strict code of ethics and conduct at all times, even in the face of adversity. It means putting the needs of the mission and the safety of others above your own personal interests or desires. And it means being willing to make sacrifices for the greater good, even if those sacrifices are painful or difficult.

For many mercenaries and PMC contractors, fulfilling the mission is not just about completing a job—it's about serving a greater purpose. Whether it's protecting innocent civilians from harm or defending the values of freedom and democracy, these individuals are driven by a sense of duty and responsibility to something larger than themselves.

But fulfilling the mission is not always easy, and it requires a great deal of skill, training, and preparation. It requires constant vigilance and attention to detail, as well as the ability to adapt to changing circumstances and unexpected challenges. And it requires a deep understanding of the risks and dangers involved, as well as the ability to mitigate those risks to ensure the safety of everyone involved.

In the end, fulfilling the mission is the ultimate goal for any mercenary or PMC contractor. It's what drives these individuals to do what they do, day in and day out, with honor, duty, and sacrifice. And it's what sets them apart from others, as they continue to serve the greater good and make a difference in the world.

Loyalty to Country and Team

Loyalty to Country and Team

In the world of mercenaries and private military contractors (PMC), loyalty is a defining characteristic. These men and women are often called upon to put their lives on the line for their country or for their team, and their unwavering commitment to their cause is what sets them apart.

For many mercenaries, loyalty to their country is the driving force behind their work. They are often former soldiers or special forces operatives who have a deep love for their homeland and a desire to serve it in any way they can. They may be called upon to undertake dangerous missions in hostile territory, risking life and limb to gather intelligence or complete a mission critical to national security.

For others, loyalty to their team is what motivates them. They may be part of a PMC that provides security services to businesses or organizations in dangerous parts of the world. In these cases, the team becomes like a family, and the bonds of loyalty and trust that develop between team members can be just as strong as those between soldiers.

Regardless of the specific circumstances, loyalty is a fundamental part of the mercenary's ethos. It is what allows them to overcome fear and adversity and to carry out their duties with honor and courage. It is also what makes them so effective in their work, as they are able to rely on their comrades and trust in their training and experience to get the job done.

Of course, loyalty is not always easy. There may be times when a mercenary is asked to undertake a mission that goes against their values or puts them in harm's way unnecessarily. In these cases, it is up to the individual to decide where their loyalties lie. Some may choose to refuse the mission or to speak out against it, while others may feel that their duty to their country or team requires them to carry out their orders regardless of personal risk or moral considerations.

Ultimately, loyalty is a complex and deeply personal concept that means different things to different people. For the mercenary, however, it is a guiding principle that shapes every aspect of their work and defines who they are as individuals. Whether they are serving their country or protecting their team, their unwavering commitment to their cause is what sets them apart and makes them true heroes of the modern age.

The Mercenary's Legacy: Tales of Honor, Duty and Sacrifice

Ethical Dilemmas

Ethical Dilemmas

As a mercenary or private military contractor (PMC), you may find yourself facing ethical dilemmas that can be difficult to navigate. These situations can arise in a variety of contexts, from deciding whether to engage in certain operations to determining how to treat detainees or civilians.

One common ethical dilemma for mercenaries and PMCs is the tension between loyalty to their employer and loyalty to their country or personal values. In some cases, a mercenary may be asked to carry out actions that conflict with their sense of morality or violate international laws. This can include engaging in torture or other forms of abuse, or targeting civilians or non-combatants.

Another common ethical dilemma is the issue of accountability. Mercenaries and PMCs often operate outside of traditional military structures, which can make it difficult to hold them accountable for their actions. This can create a situation where individuals are able to act with impunity, without fear of consequences for their actions.

Finally, there is the question of legality. Mercenaries and PMCs often operate in a legal grey area, where their actions may not be clearly defined or regulated. This can create a situation where individuals are forced to make difficult decisions without clear guidance or legal protection.

Despite these challenges, it is possible to navigate ethical dilemmas in a way that upholds the values of honor, duty, and sacrifice. This requires a commitment to transparency and accountability, as well as a willingness to engage in difficult conversations about the challenges and limitations of mercenary work.

Ultimately, the key to navigating ethical dilemmas as a mercenary or PMC is to remain focused on your mission and your values. By staying true to yourself and your sense of duty, you can ensure that your actions are always in line with your beliefs and your commitment to serving others.

The Importance of Duty

The Importance of Duty

Duty is a word that has a very special meaning for mercenaries and private military contractors (PMC). It is not just a word in a dictionary or a concept to be discussed in a classroom. Duty is an intrinsic part of their lives, their work, and their legacy.

But what is duty? Duty is the responsibility that one has towards a mission, a client, a team, and oneself. It is the obligation to act with integrity, professionalism, and courage, even in the face of danger, adversity, or moral dilemmas. Duty is what separates the mercenaries from the mercenaries, the professionals from the amateurs, and the heroes from the villains.

The importance of duty cannot be overstated. Without duty, a mercenary or a PMC would be no different than a criminal or a thug. They would have no moral compass, no sense of purpose, no loyalty, and no honor. They would be mercenaries in name only, not in spirit.

Duty is what motivates mercenaries and PMC to take on the most challenging and dangerous missions, to work long hours in hostile environments, to endure physical and emotional stress, and to put their lives on the line for their clients and their comrades.

Duty is what keeps mercenaries and PMC accountable for their actions, their decisions, and their consequences. It is what prevents them from crossing the line between lawful and unlawful, ethical and unethical, honorable and dishonorable. It is what distinguishes them from the enemies they fight against.

Duty is what creates a legacy for mercenaries and PMC. A legacy of honor, duty, and sacrifice. A legacy that inspires others to follow in their footsteps, to uphold their values, and to continue their mission. A legacy that endures beyond their lives and their careers.

In conclusion, duty is not just a word, it is a way of life for mercenaries and PMC. It is what defines them, drives them, and distinguishes them from others. It is what makes them the best of the best, the elite of the elite, and the heroes of the modern era. Duty is their legacy, and it is what they will be remembered for.

Chapter 5: The Ultimate Sacrifice

Fallen Mercenaries

Fallen Mercenaries

The life of a mercenary is not an easy one. It requires a level of mental and physical resilience that few possess. Private military contractors (PMCs) are often the first line of defense in conflict zones, tasked with protecting high-value targets and providing security for vital infrastructure. For many, the lure of adventure, the opportunity to serve their country, and the financial rewards of the job are too great to ignore.

However, with the risks come the tragic losses that are all too common in the line of duty. The fallen mercenaries are the ones who gave their lives in service of their country and the people they were protecting. They are the ones who made the ultimate sacrifice, leaving behind loved ones and families who will forever be grateful for their service.

The fallen mercenaries often come from all walks of life, united by a common desire to serve their country and make a difference. They are soldiers, sailors, airmen, and marines who have chosen to take their skills and expertise into the private sector. They are men and women who have been trained to handle the most treacherous and challenging missions, often in some of the most dangerous parts of the world.

The stories of the fallen mercenaries are often filled with bravery, courage, and selflessness. These individuals knew the risks of their job but chose to do it anyway, knowing that their services were vital to the success of their missions. Their actions often go unnoticed, but they are the ones who make the difference in the outcome of conflicts.

The legacy of the fallen mercenaries is one of honor, duty, and sacrifice. Their names may not be known to the general public, but they are respected and revered by those who knew them, and their sacrifice will never be forgotten. They are the ones who gave their lives so that others could live in peace and security.

The Mercenary's Legacy: Tales of Honor, Duty and Sacrifice

In conclusion, the fallen mercenaries are the unsung heroes of the private military contractor (PMC) industry. They are the ones who have given everything in service of their country and the people they were protecting. They will forever be remembered for their bravery, courage, and selflessness, and their legacy will continue to inspire future generations of mercenaries to follow in their footsteps.

Memorializing the Fallen

Memorializing the Fallen

In the world of mercenaries and private military contractors (PMC), the ultimate sacrifice is not uncommon. The nature of their work brings them to the forefront of some of the most dangerous and volatile situations, where the line between life and death is often blurred. But even in the face of such adversity, these brave men and women continue to put themselves at risk for the greater good. It is only fitting that we pay our respects to those who have fallen in the line of duty.

Memorializing the fallen is a tradition that dates back to ancient times. The practice of commemorating those who have given their lives in service to their country or cause is an essential part of any military or mercenary organization. The act of remembrance not only honors the memory of those who have made the ultimate sacrifice but also serves as a reminder to those who continue to serve that their efforts are not in vain.

For mercenaries and PMC's, the process of memorializing the fallen can take many forms. Some organizations have dedicated sections of their websites or social media pages to honor those who have passed away. Others have erected memorials or monuments in their honor, often featuring their names and the dates of their service. Still, others hold annual events or ceremonies to remember their fallen comrades.

The importance of memorializing the fallen cannot be overstated. It serves as a reminder to all of us of the dangers that these brave men and women face every day. It is a testament to their courage, bravery, and selflessness, and it is a reminder of the ultimate price that some have paid for the greater good.

In conclusion, memorializing the fallen is an essential part of any mercenary or PMC organization. It honors the memory of those who have made the ultimate sacrifice and serves as a reminder to those who continue to serve that their efforts are not in vain. As we remember those who have fallen, let us also take the time to honor those who continue to serve, for they are the true heroes of our time.

Impact on Families and Communities

The impact of mercenary work on families and communities is a topic that cannot be ignored. Private military contractors (PMC) and mercenaries often work in high-risk zones, where they are exposed to danger every day. This creates stress and anxiety for their families, who are left behind to worry about their loved ones' safety.

The families of PMC and mercenaries often have to deal with the uncertainty of their loved ones' whereabouts and the possibility of not being able to contact them for extended periods. This can lead to feelings of loneliness and isolation, which can have a significant impact on their mental health and wellbeing.

Moreover, when a mercenary or PMC is injured or killed while on duty, their families are left to deal with the emotional and financial consequences. Many of these contractors do not receive the same benefits as regular military personnel, which can leave their families struggling to make ends meet.

Communities where PMC and mercenaries operate can also be impacted. These individuals often work in conflict zones, where violence and instability are prevalent. Their presence can attract unwanted attention and make the community a target for attacks.

Moreover, the actions of some mercenary groups can have a negative impact on the local population. There have been reports of PMC and mercenaries engaging in human rights violations, looting, and other criminal activities. This can damage the relationship between the contractors and the local community, making it difficult for them to work together effectively.

Despite these challenges, many PMC and mercenaries take great pride in their work, seeing themselves as defenders of freedom and justice. They believe that their work is essential in protecting innocent people and preventing conflicts from escalating.

In conclusion, the impact of mercenary work on families and communities cannot be ignored. PMC and mercenaries operate in high-risk zones, which can create stress and anxiety for their loved ones. Furthermore, their presence can have a negative impact on the local community if they engage in unethical behavior. However, many contractors take great pride in their work and believe that they are making a positive difference in the world.

Legacy of Sacrifice

The legacy of sacrifice is an integral part of the world of mercenaries and private military contractors (PMC). These individuals are often tasked with some of the most dangerous and difficult missions, and as a result, they must be willing to put their lives on the line for their country or organization.

The legacy of sacrifice is not only about the willingness to risk one's life, but also about the willingness to make personal sacrifices. Many mercenaries and PMC contractors spend long periods of time away from their families, missing important milestones such as birthdays and anniversaries. They also face the challenge of developing relationships with people who may not understand the nature of their work or the sacrifices they make.

However, the legacy of sacrifice is not only about the personal sacrifices made by these individuals. It is also about the sacrifices they make for the greater good. Many mercenary and PMC contractors are involved in missions that are designed to protect innocent civilians and restore peace to areas that have been ravaged by conflict. These individuals put themselves in harm's way to ensure that others can live in safety and security.

The legacy of sacrifice is also about the impact that these individuals have on the world. Many mercenaries and PMC contractors have played important roles in shaping history, whether through their actions on the battlefield or their contributions to peacekeeping missions. Their sacrifices have helped to create a safer and more stable world.

In conclusion, the legacy of sacrifice is an essential part of the world of mercenaries and private military contractors. These individuals are willing to put their lives on the line for their country or organization, and they make personal sacrifices to ensure the success of their missions. Their sacrifices have a profound impact on the world, and their legacy is one of honor, duty, and sacrifice.

Chapter 6: The Future of the Mercenary Industry

Changes in the Industry

Changes in the Industry

The world of mercenaries and private military contractors (PMC) has gone through significant changes in recent years. These changes have been driven by a variety of factors, including shifts in global politics, advances in technology, and changes in the nature of conflict.

One of the most significant changes in the industry has been the growing use of technology. Advancements in drones, surveillance equipment, and other high-tech devices have made it easier for PMC companies to collect intelligence and carry out operations. This has also led to a shift in the types of missions that PMC companies are taking on. Rather than simply providing security for high-risk individuals or facilities, PMC companies are now increasingly involved in intelligence gathering, cyber security, and other areas that require a high degree of technical expertise.

Another major change in the industry has been the increasing use of contractors by governments around the world. This has been driven in part by pressure to reduce the number of troops deployed in conflict zones, as well as by the desire to have more flexibility in the types of operations that can be carried out. As a result, PMC companies are now playing an increasingly important role in military operations in places like Iraq, Afghanistan, and Syria.

At the same time, there has been a growing concern about the use of contractors in military operations. Critics argue that the use of contractors can lead to a lack of accountability and transparency, as well as potentially putting civilian lives at risk. As a result, there have been calls for increased oversight and regulation of the industry.

Despite these challenges, the demand for PMC services is likely to continue to grow in the coming years. As the nature of conflict continues to evolve, governments and other organizations will need to rely on PMC companies to provide a range of specialized services. At the same time, the industry will continue to face scrutiny and criticism, and companies will need to work hard to maintain their reputation and ensure that they are operating in a responsible and ethical manner.

In conclusion, the world of mercenaries and private military contractors is constantly evolving, with new challenges and opportunities arising all the time. As such, it is important for those in the industry to stay up-to-date with the latest developments and trends, and to be prepared to adapt to changing circumstances in order to remain competitive and effective.

Regulation and Oversight

Regulation and Oversight in the World of Mercenaries and Private Military Contractors

The world of mercenaries and private military contractors (PMCs) is a complex and often misunderstood one. These individuals and organizations provide a range of services to governments, corporations, and other entities around the world, from security and training to intelligence gathering and combat support. However, the lack of clear regulation and oversight in this industry has led to concerns about accountability, transparency, and even the legality of some of these activities.

One of the main challenges with regulating the activities of mercenaries and PMCs is the fact that they often operate in conflict zones or other areas where the rule of law is weak or non-existent. This can make it difficult for governments and other authorities to monitor their activities and ensure that they are acting in accordance with international law and human rights standards. In some cases, these individuals and organizations have been accused of engaging in activities that violate these norms, such as torture, extrajudicial killings, and other human rights abuses.

To address these concerns, there have been various efforts over the years to establish a framework for regulating the activities of mercenaries and PMCs. One of the most significant of these is the International Code of Conduct for Private Security Service Providers (ICoC), which was developed through a multi-stakeholder process involving governments, industry representatives, and civil society organizations. The ICoC sets out a series of principles and standards for the responsible conduct of private security companies, including requirements for human rights due diligence, transparency, and accountability.

While the ICoC has been widely adopted by many companies in the industry, there are still concerns about its effectiveness in practice. Some critics argue that the ICoC is too voluntary and lacks teeth, as there are no meaningful penalties for companies that fail to comply with its standards. Others point out that the ICoC only applies to companies that choose to sign up for it, which leaves many smaller or less reputable actors operating outside its scope.

Despite these challenges, there is a growing recognition among governments, civil society organizations, and the industry itself that greater regulation and oversight are needed in this area. This includes efforts to strengthen the ICoC and other voluntary codes of conduct, as well as exploring more formal regulatory mechanisms at the national or international level. Ultimately, the goal is to ensure that the activities of mercenaries and PMCs are subject to the same standards of accountability and transparency as other actors in the security sector, and that they do not undermine human rights or the rule of law in the areas where they operate.

Advancements in Technology

Advancements in Technology

The world of mercenaries and private military contractors (PMC) is constantly evolving and adapting to the ever-changing landscape of modern warfare. Advancements in technology have played a crucial role in shaping the way these professionals operate, allowing them to be more efficient and effective on the battlefield.

One of the most significant advancements in recent years has been the use of unmanned aerial vehicles (UAVs), or drones, in combat operations. These devices have revolutionized the way reconnaissance and surveillance missions are conducted, allowing for a safer and more accurate assessment of enemy positions. Drones have also been used for targeted strikes against high-value targets, minimizing the risk to ground forces.

Another key technological advancement is the use of advanced weapons systems. From precision-guided munitions to advanced rifles and handguns, the modern mercenary or PMC has access to a range of cutting-edge weaponry that gives them a significant advantage over their adversaries. These weapons are designed to be lightweight, easy to use, and highly effective, making them ideal for use in combat situations.

In addition to weapons and UAVs, modern mercenaries and PMCs also rely heavily on communication technology. Advanced satellite phones, radios, and other communication devices allow for real-time coordination and collaboration between team members, regardless of their location. This level of connectivity has proven to be invaluable in combat situations, where split-second decisions can mean the difference between life and death.

Finally, advancements in medical technology have also played a significant role in the world of mercenaries and PMCs. From advanced first-aid kits to portable medical facilities, these professionals have access to the tools and equipment needed to provide life-saving treatment in the field. This has greatly increased the chances of survival for those injured in combat, and has allowed for a more efficient and effective response to medical emergencies.

Overall, the advancements in technology have greatly enhanced the capabilities of modern mercenaries and PMCs, allowing them to operate more effectively and efficiently in the field. As technology continues to evolve, it is sure to play an even greater role in shaping the future of warfare and the role of these professionals in it.

Opportunities and Challenges

Opportunities and Challenges

The world of mercenaries and private military contractors (PMC) is a challenging and dynamic one, full of opportunities and potential pitfalls. For those who choose to enter this often-controversial field, the rewards can be great, but so too can the risks.

One of the key opportunities for mercenaries and PMCs is the chance to work on a wide variety of missions and projects around the world. From providing security for high-profile individuals or companies to serving as advisors and trainers for foreign militaries, there is no shortage of work for those with the necessary skills and experience.

Another major advantage of working as a mercenary or PMC is the potential for high pay and other benefits. Many private military companies offer competitive salaries, bonuses, and other incentives to attract top talent, and the work can often be lucrative for those who are successful in their missions.

However, with these opportunities come a number of challenges and potential pitfalls. One of the biggest challenges facing mercenaries and PMCs is the often-controversial nature of their work. Many people view these companies as being responsible for the rise of modern-day mercenaries, and there is often criticism leveled at their methods and tactics.

Another challenge facing mercenaries and PMCs is the risk of injury or death on the job. Many of the missions undertaken by these companies are dangerous and require a high degree of skill and experience, and the potential for harm is always present.

Finally, there is the challenge of maintaining professionalism and ethical standards in a field that is often mired in controversy and criticism. Many mercenaries and PMCs pride themselves on their honor, duty, and sacrifice, but it can be difficult to maintain these ideals in the face of intense pressure and scrutiny.

Despite these challenges, the world of mercenaries and PMCs remains an exciting and rewarding one for those who are willing to take on the risks and challenges involved. Whether you are a seasoned veteran or a newcomer to the field, there is always something new to learn and experience in this dynamic and ever-changing world.

Chapter 7: Conclusion: Reflections on the Legacy of Mercenaries

The Role of Mercenaries in History

Throughout history, mercenaries have played a vital role in shaping the outcomes of wars and conflicts. These hired soldiers, who fight for financial gain rather than patriotism or loyalty, have been used by nations, empires, and rulers to supplement their armies or as a means of waging wars without directly involving their own troops.

The use of mercenaries dates back to ancient times, where they were commonly employed by Greek city-states and Roman emperors. During the Middle Ages, mercenaries were often used by European monarchs to fight wars against one another, or as a means of suppressing rebellions and uprisings.

One of the most infamous examples of mercenaries in history is the Swiss Guard. Established in 1506, the Swiss Guard was a mercenary force hired by the Pope to protect the Vatican. Despite being a small force, the Swiss Guard has become one of the most recognizable and respected military units in the world, known for their discipline, loyalty, and bravery.

In more recent times, mercenaries have been used extensively in conflicts around the world, particularly in Africa and the Middle East. Private military contractors (PMC) mercenaries, in particular, have become increasingly popular in the 21st century, with many governments and corporations outsourcing their security needs to these private armies.

While mercenaries have often been viewed with suspicion and distrust, they have also been praised for their professionalism and effectiveness on the battlefield. In many cases, mercenaries have been able to achieve victories that would have been impossible for regular armies to accomplish.

However, the use of mercenaries has also been criticized for a number of reasons. Many argue that mercenaries lack the sense of duty and loyalty that regular soldiers possess, and that they are more prone to commit war crimes and atrocities. Others argue that the use of mercenaries undermines the sovereignty of nations, as it allows foreign powers to intervene in conflicts that do not directly involve them.

Despite these criticisms, the role of mercenaries in history cannot be ignored. From the Swiss Guard to modern PMC mercenaries, these soldiers have played a significant role in shaping the world we live in today. Whether viewed as heroes or villains, mercenaries have left a lasting legacy on the battlefield.

Lessons Learned from Mercenaries

Lessons Learned from Mercenaries

Mercenaries have been around for centuries, and while some may view them as ruthless killers, they often have valuable lessons to teach us. Private military contractors (PMC) mercenaries are one such group, and their experiences provide insight into the world of combat and the sacrifices that must be made to succeed.

One of the primary lessons to be learned from mercenaries is the importance of adaptability. These soldiers are often dropped into unfamiliar and hostile environments, and they must be able to quickly adapt to the situation at hand. This requires a high degree of mental and physical flexibility, as well as the ability to think on their feet.

Another lesson that can be learned from mercenaries is the importance of teamwork. In combat situations, there is no room for individualism or egos. PMC mercenaries understand that success is a team effort, and they work together to achieve their goals. They also understand the importance of trust and rely on each other to watch their backs.

Mercenaries also teach us the value of perseverance. In a combat situation, things can go wrong quickly, and it's easy to become overwhelmed. PMC mercenaries understand that giving up is not an option, and they push through even when the odds are stacked against them.

Finally, mercenaries teach us the importance of sacrifice. Life as a mercenary is not easy, and these soldiers often put their lives on the line for their country or cause. They understand that the greater good is more important than their individual lives, and they are willing to make sacrifices to achieve their mission.

The lessons learned from mercenaries are not just applicable to the military world. These lessons can be applied to any aspect of life, from business to personal relationships. Adaptability, teamwork, perseverance, and sacrifice are all essential qualities for success in any endeavor.

In conclusion, the lessons learned from mercenaries are invaluable. Private military contractors (PMC) mercenaries have experienced some of the most challenging situations imaginable, and their experiences provide us with valuable insights into the world of combat and the importance of teamwork, adaptability, perseverance, and sacrifice. Whether in the military or in civilian life, these lessons can help us achieve our goals and succeed in the face of adversity.

The Future of Mercenaries

The Future of Mercenaries

The world of mercenaries is changing rapidly. The rise of private military contractors (PMC) and the changing nature of warfare have created new challenges and opportunities for those who choose to work in this field.

One of the most significant changes in recent years has been the increasing use of technology in warfare. Drones, cyberattacks, and other advanced technologies have transformed the battlefield, making it easier for militaries and private contractors to conduct operations remotely. This has opened up new possibilities for mercenaries, who can now operate from anywhere in the world, using technology to carry out their missions.

Another major trend in the world of mercenaries is the increasing demand for specialized skills. As traditional military forces shrink, private contractors are being called upon to fill the gap, providing expertise in areas such as intelligence, logistics, and training. This has created new opportunities for mercenaries with specific skills and experience, such as former special forces soldiers, intelligence operatives, and engineers.

At the same time, the changing nature of warfare has also created new risks and challenges for mercenaries. The rise of non-state actors, such as terrorist groups and insurgent forces, has made it more difficult to distinguish between friend and foe. Mercenaries must be prepared to operate in complex and unpredictable environments, often with limited resources and support.

Despite these challenges, the future of mercenaries looks bright. As the world continues to evolve, the demand for skilled and experienced contractors is likely to grow. Whether working for governments or private companies, mercenaries will continue to play a vital role in shaping the future of warfare and security.

The key to success in this field will be adaptability, flexibility, and a willingness to embrace new technologies and strategies. As long as mercenaries are willing to evolve and adapt to changing circumstances, they will continue to be a valuable asset to militaries and private companies around the world.

In conclusion, the future of mercenaries is both exciting and challenging. As the world continues to change, so too must those who choose to work in this field. By staying ahead of the curve and embracing new opportunities and technologies, mercenaries can continue to make important contributions to global security and stability.

The Legacy of Mercenaries in Society.

The legacy of mercenaries in society is a complex and controversial topic that has been debated for centuries. Mercenaries, also known as private military contractors (PMC), have a long and storied history that dates back to ancient times. Despite the negative connotations associated with their line of work, mercenaries have played a vital role in shaping society as we know it.

One of the most significant contributions of mercenaries to society has been their ability to bring stability to regions plagued by conflict. In many cases, governments lack the resources and manpower to quell uprisings and maintain order. Mercenaries offer a cost-effective solution that allows nations to address security concerns without breaking the bank. This has been particularly true in Africa, where PMC's have been instrumental in maintaining peace and stability in some of the continent's most volatile regions.

The Mercenary's Legacy: Tales of Honor, Duty and Sacrifice

Another legacy of mercenaries in society is their impact on the development of modern warfare. Mercenaries have a unique perspective on warfare that can only be gained through years of experience on the front lines. They bring a level of expertise that is simply unmatched by traditional military forces. As a result, many governments have turned to PMC's to train their soldiers and develop new tactics and strategies that are better suited for modern warfare.

Despite these positive contributions, the legacy of mercenaries in society is not without controversy. Many people view them as hired guns who are more concerned with making a profit than serving their country. This perception has been fueled by high-profile incidents where PMC's have been accused of committing human rights abuses and other crimes. Critics argue that the use of mercenaries undermines the legitimacy of governments and weakens the rule of law.

In conclusion, the legacy of mercenaries in society is a complex issue that has both positive and negative aspects. While they have played a vital role in maintaining peace and stability in some of the world's most volatile regions, they have also been accused of committing human rights abuses and other crimes. As society continues to evolve, it is likely that the role of mercenaries will continue to be debated and scrutinized by both supporters and critics alike.

www.ingramcontent.com/pod-product-compliance
Lightning Source LLC
Chambersburg PA
CBHW050441010526
44118CB00013B/1634